Mezzo-Soprano/Belter Volume
Accompaniment CDs

Revised Edition

T·H·E
SINGERS
MUSICALTHEATRE
ANTH
OLOGY

A collection of songs from the musical stage, categorized by voice type. The selections are presented in their authentic settings, excerpted from the original vocal scores.

ISBN-13: 978-0-634-06201-8
ISBN-10: 0-634-06201-8

HAL•LEONARD®
CORPORATION

7777 W. BLUEMOUND RD. P.O. BOX 13819 MILWAUKEE, WI 53213

Visit Hal Leonard Online at
www.halleonard.com

DISC ONE Track List

ALLEGRO
[1] The Gentleman Is a Dope[2]

ANYONE CAN WHISTLE
[2] There Won't Be Trumpets[2]

ANYTHING GOES
[3] I Get a Kick Out of You[1]

BABES IN ARMS
[4] I Wish I Were in Love Again[4]
[5] Johnny One Note[3]

BALLROOM
[6] Fifty Percent[4]

BELLS ARE RINGING
[7] The Party's Over[4]
[8] Long Before I Knew You[2]

CHESS
[9] Someone Else's Story[4]

A CHORUS LINE
[10] What I Did for Love[3]

COMPANY
[11] Another Hundred People[2]

EVITA
[12] I'd Be Surprisingly Good for You[4]

FUNNY GIRL
[13] The Music That Makes Me Dance[3]

GOOD NEWS
[14] I Want to Be Bad[4]

GREASE
[15] Look at Me, I'm Sandra Dee[2]

GUYS AND DOLLS
[16] Adelaide's Lament[2]

GYPSY
[17] Small World[4]

HOUSE OF FLOWERS
[18] I Never Has Seen Snow[4]

I CAN GET IT FOR YOU WHOLESALE
[19] Who Knows[2]

Pianists on the CDs

[1] Brian Dean
[2] Ruben Piirainen
[3] Christopher Ruck
[4] Richard Walters

DISC TWO Track List

MAME
  [1] If He Walked into My Life[2]

ME AND JULIET
  [2] We Deserve Each Other[2]

MERRILY WE ROLL ALONG
  [3] Now You Know[2]

LES MISÉRABLES
  [4] I Dreamed a Dream[4]
  [5] On My Own[4]

THE MYSTERY OF EDWIN DROOD
  [6] The Wages of Sin[4]

NINE
  [7] My Husband Makes Movies[4]

NO STRINGS
  [8] The Sweetest Sounds[4]

OLIVER!
  [9] As Long as He Needs Me[4]

ON THE TOWN
  [10] I Can Cook Too[2]

ONCE UPON A MATTRESS
  [11] Shy[2]

PETER PAN
  [12] Never Never Land[4]

PLAIN AND FANCY
  [13] It's A Helluva Way to
       Run a Love Affair[2]

THE SECRET GARDEN
  [14] Hold On[1]

SHE LOVES ME
  [15] A Trip to the Library[4]

SONG AND DANCE
  [16] Tell Me on a Sunday[4]

**SUNDAY IN THE PARK
  WITH GEORGE**
  [17] Everybody Loves Louis[2]

THEY'RE PLAYING OUR SONG
  [18] If He Really Knew Me[2]

VICTOR/VICTORIA
  [19] Paris Makes Me Horny[2]

Pianists on the CDs
[1] Brian Dean
[2] Ruben Piirainen
[3] Christopher Ruck
[4] Richard Walters

THOUGHTS ABOUT THE ACCOMPANIMENTS AND THE SONGS

We've made every effort to choose a reasonable tempo for the recorded piano accompaniments, based on cast albums or performance precedents. Other tempos could be explored for individual interpretations. We also deliberately attempted to make the accompaniment recordings musically alive, incorporating rubato, ritardandos, accelerandos, and dynamics to inspire a theatrical performance. Nevertheless, by the very nature of recording, ours is ultimately only one interpretation.

In almost all cases we recorded the accompaniments to exactly match the editions printed in *The Singer's Musical Theatre Anthology*. It is important to point out, as a reminder, that the aim of this series is a presentation of theatre literature in its original, unchanged form. Thus, we included the entire song in the printed editions. Very occasionally, when a song felt long for a stand-alone performance or audition, we eliminated a repeat in our accompaniment recording. In those instances a first ending (or D.S.) is omitted, and the accompaniment moves directly to the final ending. For your purposes, you may choose to shorten other songs for live auditions with a pianist. A few words of caution: If this is your intention, mark the score very clearly with your cuts for the audition accompanist.

Ideally, you will be using these recorded accompaniments for practice only. Because the vocal melody is not on the recording by design, you will need to learn this at the piano or another instrument. Or if you don't play well enough to plunk through the melody of a new song, and you don't have a teacher, coach or friend to help you, you may need to seek out a recording. Some words of advice, though: You will come up with a more individual interpretation, conjured from the ground up in the manner in which all the best actors work, if you learn the song on your own, built into your unique singing voice, without imitating a recorded performance.

If you are working on a duet, it is very important that you study not only your own part, but the other singer's part as well. Then you will be ready to handle any missed entrance or mistake that he or she might make in a performance, or any improvisation that comes up, and keep things on an even keel.

Choosing the right song for you and your talents is crucial in theatre music. While all actors want to stretch beyond their "type," it is important for public performances and auditions for you to know what you can do well. There are as many theories about audition literature as there are directors. But all would agree that they want to hear you at your best, not attempting something that for some reason you feel you should do, but is not your strong suit.

There are general vocal guidelines for voice types in theatre music, but these are not in stone. A soprano with a good belt may be able to sing songs from the Soprano volumes as well as the Belter volumes. Belters may work on their "head voice" in Soprano songs. Men who have voices that lie between Tenor and Baritone, commonly called "baritenors," may find songs in both the Tenor and Baritone/Bass volumes. If you have the luxury of being able to transpose music, either through your own abilities or the help of someone else, you might consider taking a song to a different key to suit your voice. Of course, the recorded accompaniments are in only the original show keys, so they won't help you in that situation.

Recording what sometimes seemed like an endless number of piano accompaniments for *The Singer's Musical Theatre Anthology* was a mammoth task. My thanks to the pianists, assistant producers and engineers who worked so graciously with me. I especially thank Brian Dean and Christopher Ruck for their committed and sustained efforts in achieving the finished results.

Surely, with hundreds of songs from a century of shows, in multiple volumes in authentic editions, any singing actor can find several songs for any occasion. Break a leg!

Richard Walters
Series Editor and Producer

ABOUT THE ENHANCED CDs

In addition to piano accompaniments playable on both your CD player and computer, these enhanced CDs also include tempo adjustment and transposition software for computer use only. This software, known as Amazing Slow Downer, was originally created for use in pop music to allow singers and players the freedom to independently adjust both tempo and pitch elements. Because we believe there may be valuable educational use for these features in classical and theatre music, we have included this software as a tool for both the teacher and student. For quick and easy installation instructions of this software, please see below.

In recording a piano accompaniment we necessarily must choose one tempo. Our choice of tempo, phrasing, *ritardandos*, and dynamics is carefully considered. But by the nature of recording, it is only one option.

However, we encourage you to explore your own interpretive ideas, which may differ from our recordings. This new software feature allows you to adjust the tempo up and down without affecting the pitch. Likewise, Amazing Slow Downer allows you to shift pitch up and down without affecting the tempo. We recommend that these new tempo and pitch adjustment features be used with care and insight. Ideally, you will be using these recorded accompaniments and Amazing Slow Downer for practice only.

The audio quality may be somewhat compromised when played through the Amazing Slow Downer. This compromise in quality will not be a factor in playing the CD audio track on a normal CD player or through another audio computer program.

INSTALLATION INSTRUCTIONS:

For Macintosh OS 8, 9 and X:
• Load the CD-ROM into your CD-ROM Drive on your computer.
• Each computer is set up a little differently. Your computer may automatically open the audio CD portion of this enhanced CD and begin to play it.
• To access the CD-ROM features, double-click on the data portion of the CD-ROM
  (which will have the Hal Leonard icon in red and be named as the book).
• Double-click on the "Amazing OS 8 (9 or X)" folder.
• Double-click "Amazing Slow Downer"/"Amazing X PA" to run the software from the CD-ROM,
  or copy this file to your hard disk and run it from there.
• Follow the instructions on-screen to get started. The Amazing Slow Downer should display tempo, pitch and mix bars. Click to select your track and adjust pitch or tempo by sliding the appropriate bar to the left or to the right.

For Windows:
• Load the CD-ROM into your CD-ROM Drive on your computer.
• Each computer is set up a little differently. Your computer may automatically open the audio CD portion of this enhanced CD and begin to play it.
• To access the CD-ROM features, click on My Computer then right click on the Drive that you placed the CD in. Click Open. You should then see a folder named "Amazing Slow Downer". Click to open the "Amazing Slow Downer" folder.
• Double-click "setup.exe" to install the software from the CD-ROM to your hard disk. Follow the on-screen instructions to complete installation.
• Go to "Start," "Programs" and find the "Amazing Slow Downer" folder. Go to that folder and select the "Amazing Slow Downer" software.
• Follow the instructions on-screen to get started. The Amazing Slow Downer should display tempo, pitch and mix bars. Click to select your track and adjust pitch or tempo by sliding the appropriate bar to the left or to the right.
• Note: On Windows NT, 2000 and XP, the user should be logged in as the "Administrator" to guarantee access to the CD-ROM drive. Please see the help file for further information.

MINIMUM SYSTEM REQUIREMENTS:

For Macintosh:
Power Macintosh; Mac OS 8.5 or higher; 4 MB Application RAM; 8x Multi-Session CD-ROM drive

For Windows:
Pentium, Celeron or equivalent processor; Windows 95, 98, ME, NT, 2000, XP; 4 MB Application RAM; 8x Multi-Session CD-ROM drive

Also Available
THE SINGER'S MUSICAL THEATRE ANTHOLOGY

Mezzo-Soprano/Belter, Volume 1
Revised Edition
Book – HL00361072
Accompaniment CDs – HL00740230

ANNIE GET YOUR GUN
I Got the Sun in the Morning
Doin' What Comes Natur'lly

ANYONE CAN WHISTLE
Anyone Can Whistle

BABES IN ARMS
The Lady is a Tramp

CABARET
Don't Tell Mama
What Would You Do?
Cabaret

CALL ME MADAM
The Hostess with the Mostes' on the Ball

CATS
Memory

CHICAGO
Funny Honey

A CHORUS LINE
Dance: Ten; Looks: Three

CINDERELLA
Stepsisters' Lament

EVITA
Don't Cry for Me Argentina

FINIAN'S RAINBOW
How Are Things in Glocca Morra?
Look to the Rainbow

FLOWER DRUM SONG
I Enjoy Being a Girl

FOLLIES
Broadway Baby
Could I Leave You
In Buddy's Eyes
Losing My Mind

GENTLEMEN PREFER BLONDES
Diamonds Are a Girl's Best Friend
Ain't There Anyone Here for Love?

GODSPELL
Turn Back, O Man

GUYS AND DOLLS
Take Back Your Mink

GYPSY
Some People

HOW TO SUCCEED IN BUSINESS WITHOUT REALLY TRYING
Happy to Keep His Dinner Warm

KISS ME, KATE
Always True to You in My Fashion
Why Can't You Behave?

A LITTLE NIGHT MUSIC
The Miller's Son
Send in the Clowns

OKLAHOMA!
I Cain't Say No

ON A CLEAR DAY YOU CAN SEE FOREVER
He Wasn't You
What Did I Have That I Don't Have?

SOUTH PACIFIC
A Cock-Eyed Optimist
I'm in Love with a Wonderful Guy

SWEENEY TODD
By the Sea
The Worst Pies in London

TWO BY TWO
An Old Man

THE UNSINKABLE MOLLY BROWN
I Ain't Down Yet

Also Available
THE SINGER'S MUSICAL THEATRE ANTHOLOGY

Mezzo-Soprano/Belter, Volume 3
Book – HL00740123
Accompaniment CDs – HL00740232

ANNIE GET YOUR GUN
You Can't Get a Man with a Gun
They Say It's Wonderful

THE APPLE TREE
Gorgeous

BEAUTY AND THE BEAST
A Change in Me

CABARET
So What?
Mein Herr
Maybe This Time

CHICAGO
Class
When You're Good to Mama

A CHORUS LINE
Nothing

COMPANY
The Ladies Who Lunch

COWGIRLS
Heads or Tails
Don't Call Me Trailer Trash

DO RE MI
Adventure

FOLLIES
Ah, But Underneath
Uptown, Downtown

FOOTLOOSE
Can You Find It in Your Heart?

FUNNY GIRL
Don't Rain on My Parade

GIRL CRAZY
But Not for Me

GYPSY
Everything's Coming Up Roses
Rose's Turn

I CAN GET IT FOR YOU WHOLESALE
Miss Marmelstein

**I LOVE YOU, YOU'RE PERFECT,
NOW CHANGE**
Always a Bridesmaid

IS THERE LIFE AFTER HIGH SCHOOL?
Nothing Really Happened

JEKYLL & HYDE
Someone Like You
A New Life

LEAVE IT TO ME
My Heart Belongs to Daddy

MISS SAIGON
I'd Give My Life for You

PARADE
My Child Will Forgive Me
You Don't Know This Man

RUTHLESS
Teaching Third Grade

ST. LOUIS WOMAN
I Had Myself a True Love

SIDE SHOW
Who Will Love Me as I Am?

SONG AND DANCE
Let Me Finish
Third Letter Home

SONGS FOR A NEW WORLD
Stars and the Moon

SOUTH PACIFIC
Honey Bun

SUNSET BOULEVARD
As If We Never Said Goodbye
With One Look

WORKING
Just a Housewife

YOU'RE A GOOD MAN, CHARLIE BROWN
My New Philosophy

Also Available
THE SINGER'S MUSICAL THEATRE ANTHOLOGY

Mezzo-Soprano/Belter, Volume 4
Book – HL00000394
Accompaniment CDs – HL00000398

AIDA
I Know the Truth
The Past is Another Land

ANNIE GET YOUR GUN
I Got Lost in His Arms

ASPECTS OF LOVE
Anything But Lonely

AVENUE Q
There's a Fine, Fine Line

THE BEAUTIFUL GAME
Our Kind of Love

BELLS ARE RINGING
I'm Going Back

**THE BEST LITTLE WHOREHOUSE
IN TEXAS**
Hard Candy Christmas

THE BOY FROM OZ
Don't Cry Out Loud

CHESS
Heaven Help My Heart

CHICAGO
Nowadays
Roxie

A CHORUS LINE
The Music and the Mirror

**ELEGIES FOR ANGELS, PUNKS,
AND RAGING QUEENS**
Angels, Punks, and Raging Queens

FOLLIES
I'm Still Here

THE FULL MONTY
Life with Harold

GRAND HOTEL
I Want to Go To Hollywood

GREASE
There Are Worse Things I Could Do

HAIRSPRAY
I Can Hear the Bells
Miss Baltimore Crabs

JESUS CHRIST SUPERSTAR
I Don't Know How to Love Him

THE LAST FIVE YEARS
See I'm Smiling
Still Hurting

THE LION KING
Shadowland

MONTY PYTHON'S SPAMALOT
Whatever Happened to My Part?

THE PRODUCERS
When You've Got It, Flaunt It

SONGS FOR NEW WORLD
Just One Step

A STAR IS BORN
The Man that Got Away

THOROUGHLY MODERN MILLIE
Gimme Gimme

WICKED
I'm Not That Girl
Popular
The Wizard and I

THE WILD PARTY
How Did We Come to This?
Look at Me Now

WISH YOU WERE HERE
Shopping Around

WONDERFUL TOWN
One Hundred Easy Ways